LOCAL RED BOOK

C000258331

GRAYS THURROCK

STANFORD-LE-HOPE · TILBURY

CONTENTS

Red Books *showing the way*

Every effort has been made to verify the accuracy of information in this book but the publishers cannot accept responsibility for expense or loss caused by an error or omission.

Information that will be of assistance to the user of the maps will be welcomed.

The representation on these maps of a road, track or path is no evidence of the existence of a right of way.

Street plans prepared and published by ESTATE PUBLICATIONS, Bridewell House, TENTERDEN, KENT. The Publishers acknowledge the co-operation of the local authorities of towns represented in this atlas.

Ordnance Survey This product includes mapping data licensed from Ordnance Survey® with the permission of the Controller of Her Majesty's Stationery Office.

www.ESTATE-PUBLICATIONS.co.uk

Printed by Ajanta Offset, New Delhi, India.

Legend

- Pedestrianized / Restricted Access
- Track
- Built Up Area
- Footpath
- Stream
- River
- Lock Canal
- Railway / Station
- ● Post Office
- P P+ Car Park / Park & Ride
- C Public Convenience
- ✛ Place of Worship
- → One-way Street
- i Tourist Information Centre
- ▲8 ▲8 Adjoining Pages
- Area Depicting Enlarged Centre
- Emergency Services
- Industrial Buildings
- Leisure Buildings
- Education Buildings
- Hotels etc.
- Retail Buildings
- General Buildings
- Woodland
- Orchard
- Recreation Ground
- Cemetery

AVELEY

Belhus Park Golf Course

Playing Field

Swimming & Leisure Centre

Club House

Sports Ground

Sp Grd

B1335 BY-PASS

A13

Primary School

Health Centre

STANFORD GDNS
STIFFORD RD
AVELEY

PARK LANE
PARK ROAD
BROOME PL
MARTIN ROAD
DACRE
CRESCENT WY
BLOWS COTTS
ST LENNARD ROW

Recreation Ground

SHIP LANE
P STREET

CHURCH AVENUE
CHURCH ROAD

SYCAMORES AV
CHESTER CL
ELM RD
DAVIS RD
ALFRED RD
HANFORD RD
THE ROAD
DACRE CL
ST MICHAELS ST

AVENUE
HALL
EASTERN AV
FIELD RD
THE TWINS
ARNHEM AVENUE
BEECH GRO

CRESCENT
WK
THE PARADE
HALL
KENT VIEW
LOVE LANE

Mill Field Aveley F.C.

Schools

Primary School

USK ROAD
SEVERN RD
GDNS
RAVEL
TAVEL
DRIVE
TAMAR DRIVE
SHANNON RD
PINFOLDS
WAYMANS
MERESMANS
HAYWARDS
FRANKLINS
AVENUE
WAY
NETHAN DR
MONNOW RD
MON MON
TYNE GDNS
PERRY WY
NARE RD
SWALE CL

ROMFORD ROAD

AVELEY LANE

MILL

ROWAN
GRO

BUCHANAN CL
MANOR CL SOUTH
MANOR CL
GRANGE AV
TOPLANDS AV
LOWLAN DS RD
BLENHEIM GDNS

Liby
MANOR
HIGH ROAD
ROAD
MANNING ST

Aveley

Moor Hall

Pit (dis)

Pit (dis)

Sandy Lane Farm

THAMES GATEWAY

PURFLEET

Sports Grnd

Sports & Social Club
Sports Ground

PURFLEET INDUSTRIAL PARK

KERRY AVENUE
KERRY AVENUE
JULIET WAY

THURROCK COMMERCIAL CENTER

LONDON ROAD

The Willows

Willow Cottages

SANDY
NEW ROAD
NEW ROAD

LONDON ROAD
WENNINGTON RD
B1335

Wennington Hall Farm

A13

THAMES ROAD

Aveley Marshes

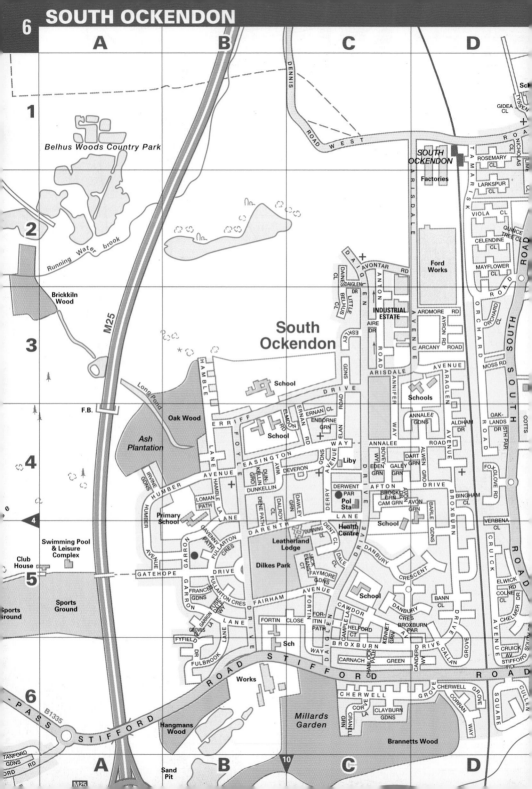

A **B** **C** **D**

1

Belhus Woods Country Park

GIDEA CL

SOUTH
OCKENDON

Factories

ROSEMARY CL

NICHOLAS CL

LARKSPUR CL

TAMARISK

2

Running Water brook

VIOLA CL

QUINCE TREE CL

CELENDINE CL

MAYFLOWER CL

Brickkiln
Wood

SOUTH ROAD

ORCHARD ROAD

DAIGLEN

AVONTAR RD

INDUSTRIAL
ESTATE

ARDMORE RD

AYRON RD

MOSS RD

ARCANY ROAD

Ford
Works

M25

3

South
Ockendon

DAINES DR

LITTLE BELHUS

AIRE DR

EASEY

ARISDALE

AVENUE

OAK-LANDS DR

ALDHAM DR

CL

COTTS

F.B.

Long Pond

Oak Wood

School

School

HAMBLE LANE

ERRIFF

FOY

ERNAN CL

ELMDON RD

ERNAN RD

ENBORNE GRN

GDNS

ROAD

ELAN

DRIVE

ANNIFER

ARAGLEN

Schools

ANNALEE GDNS

AVENUE

Ash
Plantation

IRVINE GDNS

HUMBER AVENUE

EASINGTON AVENUE

HAMBLE LA

DUNKELLIN

DUN-KELLIN GRO

DEVERON

GDNS

WAY

Liby

ANNALEE

BOVEY WY

EDEN GRN

DART CL

GALEY GRN

ALWEN GRO

ROAD

AVENUE

ALDHAM

BINGHAM CL

BARLE CL

BROXBURN

4

4

Primary
School

LOMAN PATH

DENE PATH

DALROY CL

DAWLEY GRN

DERWENT

AFTON

BROCK RD

CAM GRN

BRN

AVON GRN

Pol Sta

PAR

School

AXY

GDNS

VERBENA CL

FO GLOVE RD

CRUICK ROAD

Swimming Pool
& Leisure
Complex

Club
House

GARRON

GAVENNY PATH

FULLARTON CRES

DENT CL

Leatherland
Lodge

Dilkes Park

JACK LANE

DUNNING GDNS

DALE

DANBURY

Health
Centre

DRIVE

School

DANBURY CRES

ELWICK RD

COLNE DR

5

5

Sports
Ground

FRANCE GDNS

GARRON DRIVE

FAIRHAM

FORTIN

AVENUE

FAYMORE GDNS

CAWDOR

KENNET GRN

BROXBURN PAR

BANN CL

BAOUD DRIVE

CALLAN

CHELMER AV

CRUICK AV STIFFORD RD

GATEHOPE

GROVES

FYFIELD DR

FULBROOK

FULLARTON CRES

LANE

FORTIN CLOSE

FOR-TIN PATH

CAMPLE LA

HELFORD GRN

CARNACH

CANDERO WY

CHANLOCK PATH

GREEN

BROXBURN WAY

DAIGLEN DRIVE

GROVE

CORRAN WAY

CULLEN

Sports
Ground

B1335

BY-PASS

STIFFORD ROAD

Works

Hangmans
Wood

Millards
Garden

CHERWELL GRN

COR

CRANE LA

CLAYBURN GDNS

CHERWELL

Brannetts Wood

SQUARE

STANFORD GDNS RD

M25

Sand
Pit

10

A **B** **C** **D**

A B C D

1

Orsett Fen

Reservoir

Hobletts

Mar Dyke

2

Waste Disposal Site

7

3

age ks

LANE FEN LANE LANE

FEN LANE

4

Baker Street

7

G R E E N

ROAD HIGH RD

Windmill (disused)

S T I F F O R D   C L A Y S

BAKER STREET

5

A13

CLAYS ROAD

School

BLACKSHOTS

Grey Goose Farm

6

SILVER

PHILIP AV

STIFFORD

KINGSMAN

PRINCE   DURNINGE

GOURNEY   WY   GLADE

WHITMORE

PHILIP   CHAFFORD WAY

BRADSHAWE RD   FLEETHALL

FLEET GRO   HALFORD GRO

W. WELLINGTON

CHAFFORD WAY

CT.

CRAMMAVILL

CRAMMAVILL ST

CLAYS STIFFORD

ROAD

STIFFORD

CLAYS

GROVE

AVENUE

FAIRWAY

Stifford Clays C.P. School

ST   A

Rec Grnd

BLACKTHORN RD

OAK WAY

MEADOW RD

FAIR

LEAS

AVENUE

THE FIRS

ELM   WAY

FARM DR

FAIRFIELD   AV

ASHLEY   GARD

BROOKMANS

FOX

12

THURROCK

FARM

LANE

BLACKSH

HILL

FOX

HO

LANE   KER

KEIR HARDIE HO

Gammon Field (Travellers Site)

GAMMON FIELD

A1089

A B C D

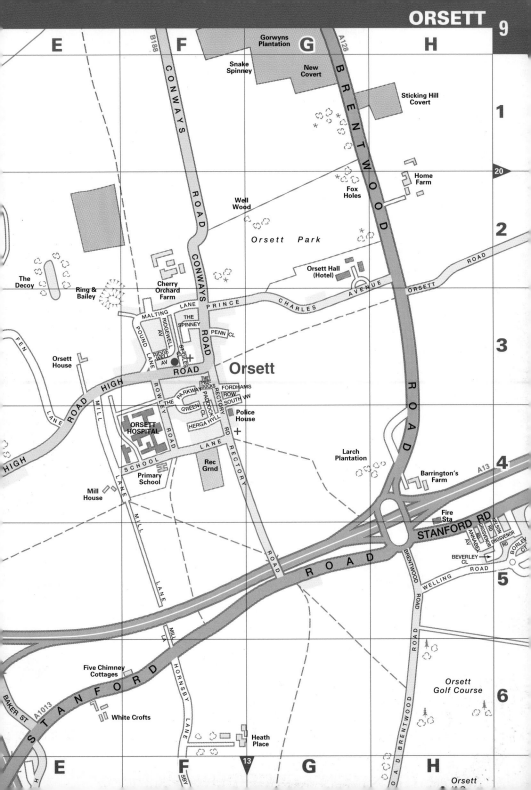

B1188

CONWAYS ROAD

Gorwyns Plantation

Snake Spinney

New Covert

BRENTWOOD

Sticking Hill Covert

Home Farm

Well Wood

Fox Holes

Orsett Park

ROAD

The Decoy

Ring & Bailey

Cherry Orchard Farm

CONWAYS LANE

Orsett Hall (Hotel)

AVENUE

CHARLES

PRINCE

ORSETT

MALTING

RIDGEWELL AV

THE SPINNEY

PENN CL

FEN

POUND LANE

RIDGE WELL AV

EGLES

ROAD

Orsett

Orsett House

HIGH

MILL LANE

ROAD

ROWLEY

THE GREEN

PARKWAY

THE PADDOCKS

PADDOCK CL

FORDHAMS ROW SOUTH VW

RECTORY

Police House

ROAD

HERGA HYLL

ORSETT HOSPITAL

SCHOOL LANE

Primary School

Rec Grnd

RECTORY

Larch Plantation

ROAD

Barrington's Farm

A13

Mill House

MILL LANE

Fire Sta

STANFORD RD

NELSON RD

ANNABEL

GROSVENOR RD

BEVERLEY CL

GROSVENOR RD

BORLEY CT

ROAD

BRENTWOOD ROAD

WELLING ROAD

Five Chimney Cottages

MILL LA

HORNSBY LANE

BAKER ST

A1013

STANFORD

White Crofts

Orsett Golf Course

Heath Place

SBY

13

Orsett

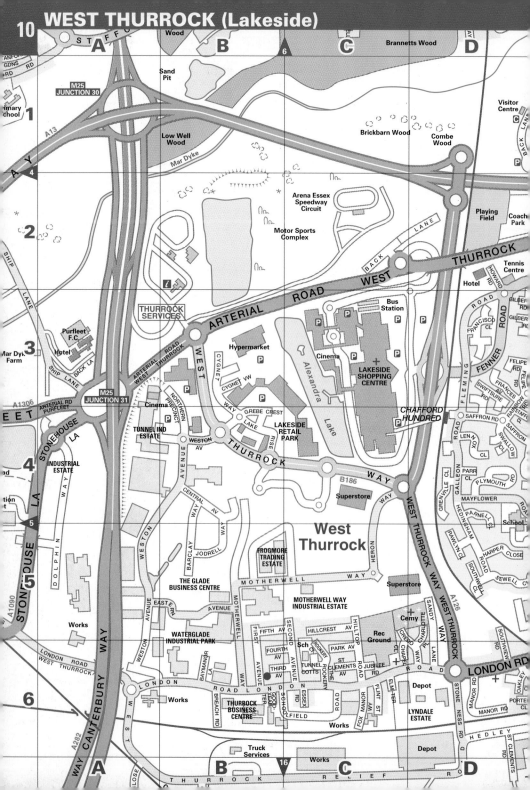

A · CONWAY · MANOR WAY · FALCON AV · ST · THAMES RD · P · CREST AV · CURZON DR · CURZON DRIVE

B

12 · **C** Little Thurro Marshes

D

P · Grays Beach Riverside Park · Boating Lake

THURROCK

SYRINGE · SEDLE · SPEED-WELL CT · DOCK APPROACH ROAD · A1089

1
Works · Mills · Finnish Terminal · Rail Container Terminal · CAPSTAN CENTRE IND EST · Supermarket · PARKWAY · ST ANDREWS · DOCK · Karting Stadium

2
Granary · Deep Sea Container Terminal · Jetty · Tilbury · Warehouses · ROAD · TOWN · Athlone House · GAYLOR · MELBOURNE RD · RUSSELL · CHURCH · SEYMOUR · ROAD

Grain Terminal · Works · Leslie Ford Ho · TENNANT'S · ROW

3
Northfleet Hope · Northfleet Hope House · Northfleet Hope Container Terminal · Docks · Custom House · West Branch Dock · Centre Branch Dock · Warehouses

4
Pier · Tower Wharf · R I V E R · Tilbury Free Port

5
Piers · Pier · Warehouses · Tilbury Ness · Warehouses · Warehouse · Jetty · Jetty

T H A M E S

6
ROAD · THE CREEK · GROVE · WALLIS PARK · COLLEGE ROAD · **Northfleet** · STONEBRIDGE RD · Huggens College · WARWICK · FISHERMENS HILL · FORD · KINGSTON · HIVE LA · LAWN · Works · THE SHORE

THE NORTH WAY · ST · ROSE ST · EBBSFLEET WK · **NORTHFLEET HIGH ST** · STA RD · STATION RD · FACTORY RD · Sch · LAWN RD · CRETE HALL ROAD

A · **B** · **C** · **D**

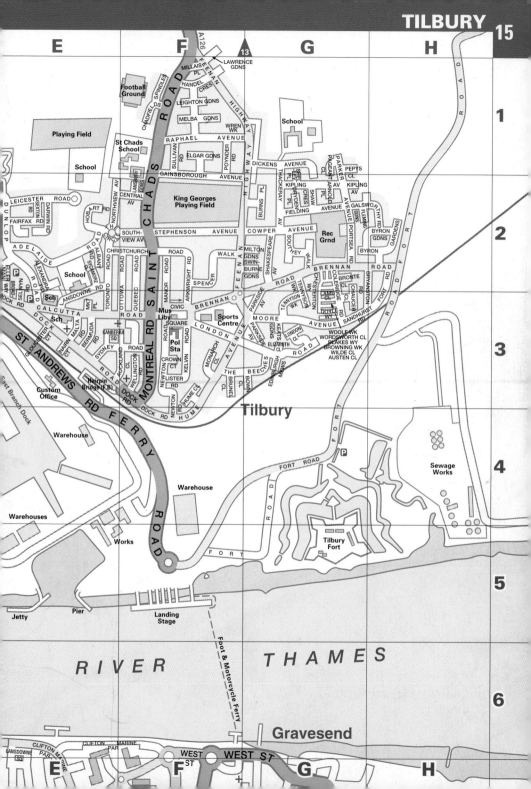

E   **F**   **G**   **H**

1

Football Ground

Playing Field

School

St Chads School

LAWRENCE GDNS

MILLAIS PL

HANDEL CRES

LEIGHTON GDNS

MELBA GDNS

WREN WK

School

RAPHAEL AVENUE

SULLIVAN RD

ELGAR GDNS

POYNDER RD

GAINSBOROUGH AVENUE

DICKENS AVENUE

PARKER CL

PEPYS CL

KIPLING AV

2

King Georges Playing Field

Leicester Road

Fairfax Rd

Darwin Rd

School

Adelaide Rd

Alexandra Rd

Calcutta Rd

Sch

Sch

School

SOUTH-VIEW AV

CHRISTCHURCH ROAD

STEPHENSON AVENUE

COWPER AVENUE

Rec Grnd

BYRON GARDENS

BYRON

SPEKE CL

KIPLING PL

DRYDEN PL

SHAW AV

FIELDING

GALSWORTHY RD

FLUXING GDNS

PORTSEA RD

BRENNAN ROAD

3

Dunlop

St Andrews Rd Ferry Road

Custom Office

Warehouse

Warehouses

Works

Montreal Rd Saint Chads Road

Albany Road

Lansdowne

MKT

CANBERRA RD

SYDNEY RD

AUCKLAND CL

WELLINGTON RD

Hairpin Bridge (F.B)

Mus Liby

CIVIC SQUARE

Pol Sta

CROWN CT

LISTER RD

NEWTON RD

KELVIN RD

HUME CT

Sports Centre

BRENNAN

MANOR ROAD

ARKWRIGHT RD

SPENCER

WALK

LONDON RD

MONARCH CL

THE BRUNEL

MOORE

PARKSIDE GDNS

KEATS CL

BOWN CL

BEECHES

EDINBURGH MEWS

ELIZABETH RD

LONDON RD

CHESTERTON WY

TENNYSON WK

TENNYSON WK

DOYLE WY

LAMB CL

BRONTE RD

CHAUCER RD

BRANSTON RD

SANDHURST RD

Road Fort

WOOLF WK
WORDSWORTH CL
BEAKES WY
BROWNING WK
WILDE CL
AUSTEN CL

Tilbury

4

Warehouse

Fort Road

P

Sewage Works

Tilbury Fort

Fort Road

5

Jetty

Pier

Landing Stage

Foot & Motorcycle Ferry

6

R I V E R   *T H A M E S*

Gravesend

CLIFTON MARINE PAR

WEST ST

WEST ST

E   **F**   **G**   **H**

A **B** **C** **D**

1

Mucking Marshes

Walton's
Hall
Museum

Caravan &
Camp Site

Works

NORTHUMBERLAND RD

ESSEX
GDNS

DORSET
GDNS

HAMP-
SHIRE
GDNS

DEVONSHIRE
GDNS

Linford

STAFFORD

LOWER CRESCENT
MEADOW

2

George &
Dragon
P.H.

Recreation
Ground

Becksland

Ashlea
Farm

HAZEL
BEECHCROFT AV
WOOD
HALT

HALT
DR
PINE
WOOD
CL

NIGH ASH
DRIVE

BRINDLES
CL

STEINING AV

*EAST
TILBURY*

ALEXANDRA
WAY

THOMAS
BATA

KING GEORGE VI AVENUE
QUEEN ELIZABETH

SEVERN

WALDON

HAYLE

BURE
SQ

DEBDENO

COLNE

COLNE
CT

WELLAND

ROMAN

TOR-
RIDGE

STRATH
MORE

CLYDE

ROACH
TYNE

CALDER

TWEED

ORWELL

CAMBOURNE AV

ARUN

TRENT

3

MUCKINGFORD

COAL

ROAD

LOW STREET LANE

COAL

ROAD

COAL

MARGARET

ROAD

**East
Tilbury**

CORONATION

CORONATION AV

AVENUE

AVENUE

QUEEN MARY AV

CORONATION AV

Liby

CORONATION
AV

PRINCESS

GLOUCESTER
AV

FARM
RD

School

4

BATA AV

Thomas
Bata
Mem
Park

PRINCESS

THAMES
INDUSTRIAL
PARK

Sports
Ground

5

**Low
Street**

Works

Gravelpit
Farm

ROAD COAL

LOVE
LANE

MARGARET
ROAD

Barvills
Farm

6

CHURCH   ROAD

STATION
RD

STATION

ROAD

STATION   ROAD

STATION   ROAD

Walnut
Tree Farm

A **B** **C** **D**

Fobbing

Corringham

Container Terminal

THE MANORWAY

A1014 MANORWAY

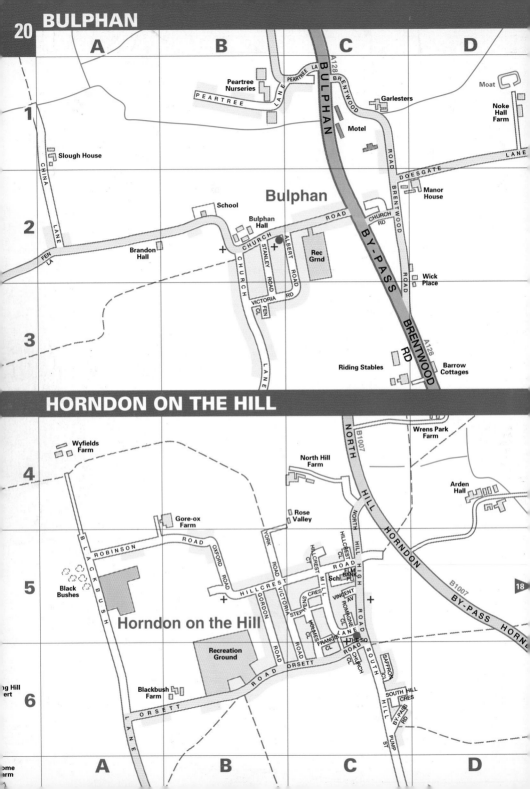

A   B   C   D

1

Peartree Nurseries

PEARTREE

PEARTREE LA

A128 BULPHAN

BRENTWOOD

Garlesters

Motel

Moat

Noke Hall Farm

LANE

Slough House

CHINA LANE

DOESGATE

BRENTWOOD ROAD

Manor House

Bulphan

School

Bulphan Hall

Bulphan ROAD

CHURCH RD

BY-PASS

2

FEN LA

Brandon Hall

CHURCH LANE

STANLEY ROAD

ALBERT ROAD

CHURCH ROAD

Rec Grnd

BRENTWOOD ROAD

Wick Place

VICTORIA RD

FEN

3

A128 BRENTWOOD RD

Riding Stables

Barrow Cottages

HORNDON ON THE HILL

A   B   C   D

Wrens Park Farm

NORTH

B1007

HILL

4

Wyfields Farm

North Hill Farm

HORNDON

Arden Hall

Gore-ox Farm

Rose Valley

NORTH HILL

ROAD

ROBINSON ROAD

OXFORD ROAD

YORK ROAD

HILLCREST CT

HILLCREST ROAD

ELM BANK PL

Sch

HIGH ROAD

B1007 BY-PASS HORNE

18

5

Black Bushes

BLACKBUSH

VICTORIA ROAD

GORDON ROAD

HILLCREST

CREST

STEPNEY

HOLMES CL

VINCENT AV

ROMAGNE

FRANCIS CL

SOUTH ROAD

Horndon on the Hill

Recreation Ground

ROAD

ROAD

CHURCH LANE

THE SQ

CHURCH

SAFFRON CL

6

Blackbush Farm

ORSETT ROAD

ORSETT LANE

SOUTH HILL CRES

HILL

BY-PASS RD

PUMP ST

ome arm

g Hill ert

A   B   C   D

The Index includes some names for which there is insufficient space on the maps. These names are indicated by an * and are followed by the nearest adjoining thoroughfare.

Juliet Way RM19	4 A4	Loewen Rd RM16	13 E3
Juniper Dr RM15	7 F2	Loman Path RM15	6 B4
Jurgens Rd RM19	5 F8	London Cl RM18	15 G3
		London Rd, Aveley RM13,15,19	4 A1
Karen Cl SS17	18 B5	London Rd,	
Kathleen Cl SS17	18 C2	Grays RM17	3 A2
Keats Gdns RM18	15 G3	London Rd,	
Keir Hardie Ho RM16	12 C1	Purfleet RM19	5 C7
Kelvin Rd RM18	15 F3	London Rd,	
Kelvinside SS17	18 D2	Stanford-le-Hope SS17	18 A6
Kempley Ct RM17	3 F2	London Rd,	
Kendale RM16	13 F3	Tilbury RM18	15 F3
Kennet Grn RM15	6 C6	London Rd,	
Kenneth Gdns SS17	18 D1	West Thurrock RM20	10 A6
Kent Rd RM17	3 E2	Long Ct RM19	5 C6
Kent Vw RM15	4 D4	Long La RM16	11 H1
Kenwood Rd SS17	19 F2	Longhouse Rd RM16	13 G3
Kerry Av RM19	4 B4	Love La,	
Kerry Rd RM16	12 C1	South Ockendon RM15	4 D4
Kersbrooke Way SS17	19 F1	Love La, Tilbury RM18	17 C6
Kershaw Cl RM16	11 E3	Low Street La RM18	17 A4
Kiln Way RM17	3 A1	Lower Cres SS17	17 B2
King Edward Dr RM16	12 D2	Lowlands Rd RM15	4 D3
King Edwards Rd SS17	18 C6	Lucas Rd RM17	11 H2
King George VI Av RM18	17 C3	Ludlow Pl RM17	12 A3
King St SS17	18 B5	Lulworth Cl SS17	18 A6
Kings Walk RM17	3 B3	**Lyndale Est RM20**	**16 E1**
Kingsley Walk RM16	13 F4	Lyndhurst Rd SS17	18 D2
Kingsman Dr RM16	8 A6	Lytton Rd RM16	13 E4
Kingsman Rd SS17	18 A5		
Kingston Ct DA11	14 A6	**M**ace Ct RM17	12 C6
Kipling Av RM18	15 G2	Mackley Dr SS17	18 D2
Knowlton Cotts RM15	6 D4	Macleod Cl RM17	12 B4
Kynoch Ct SS17	18 C5	Magnet Rd RM20	16 F1
Kyrkly Ct*,		Magnet Ter SS17	18 C5
Linnet Way RM19	5 D7	Magnolia Cl SS17	7 F2
		Magnolia Pl SS17	18 C2
Laburnum Cres SS17	19 F3	Maidstone Rd RM17	3 B2
Laburnum Dr SS17	19 F3	Mallow Ct RM17	12 C6
Laburnum Gro RM15	7 E2	Malpas Rd RM16	13 G3
Laird Av RM16	12 C1	Malta Rd RM18	15 E3
Lake Rise RM20	10 B4	Malting La RM16	9 F3
Lakeside Retail Pk RM20	**10 B4**	Malvern Rd RM17	12 C4
Lakeside Shopping Centre RM20	**10 C3**	Manning St RM15	4 E3
Lamb Cl RM18	15 G3	Manor Cl RM15	4 E3
Lambourne RM18	17 D4	Manor Cl South RM15	4 E3
Lametsdowne SS17	19 F2	Manor Rd,	
Lampits Hill SS17	19 F1	Grays RM17	3 F3
Lampits La SS17	19 F1	Manor Rd,	
Lancaster Rd RM20	11 E5	Stanford-le-Hope SS17	18 C5
Lander Rd RM17	12 C5	Manor Rd,	
Langdon Way SS17	19 E2	Tilbury RM18	15 F3
Langland Cl SS17	19 E2	Manor Rd,	
Langthorne Cres RM17	12 B4	West Thurrock RM20	16 E1
Langton Way RM16	13 G4	Manor Way,	
Lansbury Gdns RM18	15 F2	Grays RM17	3 D4
Lansdowne Rd RM18	15 E3	Manor Way,	
Lansdowne Sq DA11	18 F6	Stanford-le-Hope SS17	19 F5
Larkfield SS17	19 G1	Maple Dr RM15	7 E3
Larkspur Cl RM15	6 D2	Maple Rd RM17	3 F3
Larkswood Rd SS17	19 G2	Maples SS17	18 C4
Laurel Dr RM17	7 E2	Mar Rd RM15	7 E2
Lawn Rd DA11	14 B6	Marian Cl RM16	11 G1
Lawns Cres RM17	12 C6	Marine Ct RM19	5 B6
Lawns Pl RM17	12 C6	Marisco Cl RM16	13 F4
Lawrence Gdns RM18	15 F1	Markhams SS17	18 D4
Laxtons SS17	19 E2	Marlborough Cl RM16	12 B2
Lea Rd RM16	13 F5	Marlow Av RM19	5 B6
Leasway RM16	12 B1	Marram Ct RM17	12 C6
Leicester Rd RM18	15 E2	Marsh La SS17	19 H1
Leighton Gdns RM18	15 F1	Marshfoot Rd RM17	12 D5
Lenmore Av RM17	12 B3	Martin Rd RM15	4 E3
Lennard Row RM15	4 F3	Martins Cl SS17	18 C3
Lennox Rd RM20	10 D4	Mary Rose Cl RM20	11 E4
Lenthall Av RM17	11 H2	Masefield Rd RM16	12 D2
Lever Sq RM16	13 E4	Maunder Cl RM16	11 E4
Leveson Rd RM16	13 F3	May Ct RM17	12 C6
Levett Rd SS17	18 D5	Maycroft Av RM17	12 C5
Lewes Cl RM17	3 A3	Maycroft Gdns RM17	12 C4
Lime Cl RM15	6 D1	Mayfields RM16	12 B2
Limeslade Cl SS17	19 E2	Mayflower Cl RM15	6 D2
Linden Cl RM19	5 E7	Mayflower Rd RM20	10 D4
Linford Rd RM16	13 F4	Mead Cl RM16	12 A2
Link Rd SS17	18 C3	Meadow Cl SS17	17 B2
Linnet Way RM19	5 D7	Meadow Rd RM16	8 B6
Lion Hill SS17	19 H2	Meadway RM17	12 C3
Lisle Pl RM17	11 H2	Medebridge Rd RM16	7 G5
Lister Rd RM18	15 F3	Medick Ct RM17	12 C6
Little Belhus Cl RM15	6 C3	Medina Rd RM17	12 C4
Locke Cl SS17	18 B3	Medlar Dr RM15	7 F2
Lockyer Rd RM19	5 E7	Medlar Rd RM17	12 C6
Lodge La RM16,17	11 H1	Meesons La RM16	11 G3

Melba Gdns RM18	15 F1	Nutberry Cl RM16	11 H1
Melbourne Rd SS17	14 D2		
Meredith Rd RM16	13 E4	**O**ak Ct RM15	7 E1
Meresmans RM15	4 E1	Oak Rd RM17	3 E3
Merlin Cl RM16	11 F2	Oakhill Rd RM19	5 D7
Merton Pl RM17	13 F4	Oaklands Dr RM15	6 D4
Milford Rd RM16	12 C1	Oakley Cl RM20	16 F1
Mill La, Fobbing SS17	19 H1	Oakway RM16	8 A6
Mill La,		Oakwood Rd SS17	19 F2
Horndon on the Hill SS17	20 C5	Old Dock Approach Rd SS17	12 D4
Mill La, Orsett RM16	9 E3	Old Jenkins Cl SS17	18 A6
Mill La,		Oliver Rd RM20	16 C3
South Stifford RM16	11 E4	Orchard Cl RM15	6 D3
Mill Rd, Purfleet RM19	5 D8	Orchard Dr RM17	11 H2
Mill Rd,		Orchard Rd RM15	6 D3
South Ockendon RM15	4 D2	Orchis Gro RM15	3 A1
Millais Pl RM18	15 F1	Orsett Heath Cres RM16	13 E3
Milton Gdns RM18	15 G2	Orsett Rd,	
Milton Rd,		Grays RM17	3 B2
Grays RM17	3 C1	Orsett Rd,	
Milton Rd,		Horndon on the Hill RM16	20 A6
Stanford-le-Hope SS17	19 E1	Orsett Rd,	
Mollands Cl RM15	7 F3	Orsett RM16	9 H3
Mollands La RM15	7 F3	Orwell RM18	17 D4
Monarch Cl RM18	15 F3	Ottowa Rd RM16	15 F3
Monks Haven SS17	18 D4	Oval Gdns RM17	12 B3
Monnow Grn RM15	4 E2	Overcliff Rd RM17	12 B4
Monnow Rd RM15	4 E2	Oxford Av RM16	13 F4
Montfort Av SS17	19 F2	Oxford Rd,	
Montgomery Cl RM16	12 B1	Horndon on the Hill SS17	20 B5
Montreal Rd RM16	15 F3	Oxford Rd,	
Moore Av,		Stanford-le-Hope SS17	18 A6
Grays RM20	11 F5	Oxley Gdns SS17	18 C2
Moore Av,		Oxwich St SS17	19 E2
Tilbury RM18	15 G3		
Morant Rd RM16	13 G2	**P**addock Cl RM16	9 F3
Moreland Av RM16	12 B2	Pageant Cl RM18	15 G1
Morley Hill SS17	18 D1	Pagette Way RM17	11 H4
Morley Link SS17	18 D1	Painswick Av SS17	18 D1
Morley Sq RM16	13 F4	Palins Way RM16	11 H1
Morrison Rd RM16	12 C1	Palmers SS17	19 E1
Moss Bank RM17	11 G4	Palmers Av RM17	3 E1
Moss Rd RM15	6 D3	Palmers Dr RM17	3 E1
Motherwell Way RM20	10 B5	Palmerston Gdns RM20	11 E5
Motherwell Way Ind Est RM20	**10 C5**	Palmerston Rd RM20	11 E5
Mountfield Cl SS17	18 D3	Park Av RM20	10 C6
Muckingford Rd RM18	17 A4	Park La RM15	4 F3
Mulberry Dr RM19	5 B6	Park Mws*,	
Mullein Ct RM17	12 C6	Park La RM15	4 F3
Myrtle Gro RM15	4 D4	Park Rd,	
		Corringham SS17	19 F3
Nairn Ct RM18	15 E3	Park Rd, Grays RM17	3 D2
Nare Rd RM15	4 D2	Park Rd,	
Nelson Rd,		Stanford-le-Hope SS17	18 A5
Grays RM16	9 H4	Park View Gdns RM17	3 D1
Nelson Rd,		Park Vw RM15	4 F3
South Ockendon RM15	7 E1	Parker Av RM18	15 G1
Nethan Dr RM15	4 D2	Parker Rd RM17	11 G5
Nevell Rd RM16	13 F3	Parkmill Cl SS17	19 E2
New Rd, Grays RM17	3 C3	Parkside RM16	12 B2
New Rd, Grays RM17	3 D3	Parkside Av RM18	15 G3
New Rd,		Parkway, Grays RM16	9 F3
Rainham RM13	4 A2	Parkway,	
Newbough Rd RM17	3 F1	Stanford-le-Hope SS17	19 G2
Newnham Pl RM18	13 F4	Parnell Cl SS17	10 D4
Newton Cl SS17	19 E2	Parr Cl RM20	10 D4
Newton Rd RM18	15 F3	Parry Cl SS17	18 B3
Nicholas Cl RM15	6 D1	Parsonage Rd RM20	16 F1
Nicholas Walk RM16	13 G2	Pearsons SS17	19 E3
Nordmann Pl RM15	7 E2	Peartree Cl RM15	6 D2
Norfolk Pl RM20	11 E4	Peartree La RM14	20 B1
North Hill SS17	20 C4	Pelham Pl SS17	18 C2
North Rd,		Pembroke Av RM17	19 F2
Purfleet RM19	5 D6	Pendine Cl SS17	19 E2
North Rd,		Penn Cl RM16	9 F3
South Ockendon RM15	7 E1	Penny La SS17	19 F2
Northern Precinct RM20	10 B3	Pepys Rd RM18	15 G1
Northfields RM17	12 B4	Percy St RM17	3 E3
Northlands SS17	18 D1	Perry Way RM15	4 E2
Northolme Cl RM16	12 B2	Philippa Way RM16	13 G3
Northumberland Rd SS17	17 A2	Phillip Sydney Rd RM20	11 E5
Northview Av RM18	15 E2	Piggs Cnr RM17	12 B3
Northwood RM16	13 G2	Pilgrims La RM15	11 E1
Norton Cl SS17	19 E1	Pinewood Cl RM18	13 G2
Nottage Cl SS17	19 E2	Pinfolds RM15	4 E1
Nunns Way RM17	12 C6	Plaistow Cl SS17	18 C4
Nursery Gdns RM15	7 E2	Plashet Cl SS17	18 C4
Nursery Rd SS17	12 D1	Plymouth Rd RM20	10 D4
Nutberry Av RM16	12 A1	Poley Rd RM15	4 E1

Poole Ho RM16	13 G2
Poplar Cl RM15	7 F2
Porter Cl RM20	16 F1
Portsea Rd RM18	15 G2
Pound La RM16	9 F3
Poynder Rd RM18	15 F1
Premier Av RM16	12 B2
Priestley Ct RM17	12 B4
Prince Charles Av RM16	9 F3
Prince Philip Av RM16	7 H6
Princes Av SS17	19 F3
Princes Av RM18	17 C4
Princess Margaret Rd RM18	17 B2
Prior Chase RM17	11 H4
Priory Rd SS17	18 D4
Prospect Av SS17	18 A6
Prospect Pl RM17	3 D3
Pugh Pl SS17	18 C2
Pump St SS17	20 C6
Purcell Cl SS17	18 B4
Purcell Way SS17	18 B4
Purfleet By-Pass RM19	5 D6
Purfleet Ind. Pk RM15	**4 B4**
Purfleet Rd RM15	4 B4
Pym Pl RM17	11 H4
Quarry Hill RM17	3 B2
Quarry Mws RM19	5 C6
Quebec Rd RM18	15 F3
Queen Elizabeth Av RM18	17 C3
Queen Elizabeth Dr SS17	19 E1
Queen Mary Av RM18	17 C4
Queensgate Centre RM17	**3 C2**
Quince Tree Cl RM15	6 D2
Rachael Clarke Cl SS17	18 D2
Rainbow La SS17	18 D5
Rainbow Rd RM16	10 D4
Raphael Av RM18	15 F1
Rapier Cl RM19	5 B6
Ravel Gdns RM15	4 E1
Ravel Rd RM15	4 E1
Ravenscroft RM16	13 G2
Rawlyn Cl RM20	10 D5
Rayleigh Rd SS17	18 A5
Recreation Av SS17	19 G2
Rectory Rd,	
Orsett RM16	9 F3
Rectory Rd,	
Sockett's Heath RM17	12 C3
Rectory Rd,	
Stanford-le-Hope SS17	18 B6
Rectory Ter SS17	18 B5
Redbrooke Ct SS17	17 B2
Redlie Cl SS17	18 C3
Redwood Chase RM15	7 E2
Regan Cl SS17	18 D2
Regent Cl RM16	12 B2
Richmond Rd RM17	3 E2
Ridgeway RM17	12 C3
Ridgewell Av RM16	9 F3
Rigby Gdns RM16	13 F4
River Ct RM19	5 B6
River Vw RM16	13 E4
Riverview Flats*,	
Linnet Way RM19	5 D7
Roach RM18	17 D3
Robinson Rd RM16	20 A5
Rodings Av SS17	19 G3
Rogers Rd RM17	12 B3
Romagne Cl SS17	20 C5
Roman RM18	17 D3
Romford Rd RM15	4 D2
Romsey Cl SS17	18 A5
Rookery Cl SS17	18 A5
Rookery Ct RM20	10 C6
Rookery Ct*,	
Linnet Way RM19	5 D7
Rookery Hill SS17	19 G3
Rookery La RM17	12 C5
Rookery Vw RM17	12 C5
Rookwood Cl RM17	12 A4
Rose Valley Cres SS17	18 C2
Roseberry Rd RM17	11 G5
Rosedale Rd RM17	12 C4
Rosemary Cl RM15	6 D1
Rosewood Cl RM15	7 F2
Rowan Gro RM15	4 F3

23

Rowan Way RM15 7 E2
Rowley Rd RM16 9 F3
Runnymede Rd SS17 18 B5
Rushdon Rd RM17 11 H3
Rushley Cl RM16 12 C1
Ruskin Rd,
  Grays RM16 13 E4
Ruskin Rd,
  Stanford-le-Hope
  SS17 18 A5
Russel Rd RM18 11 H4
Russell Rd RM18 14 D2
Russet Cl SS17 18 B3
Ryde Cl SS17 18 B6
Rykhill RM16 13 G2

Saffron Cl SS17 20 C6
Saffron Rd RM16 10 D4
St Andrews Rd RM18 14 D1
St Annes Cl RM16 12 A1
St Augustine Rd
  RM16 13 G4
St Cecilias Rd RM16 13 G4
St Chads Rd RM17,18 15 F3
St Clements Av RM20 10 C6
St Clements Ct RM19 5 C6
St Clements Rd RM20 16 F2
St Francis Way RM16 13 G3
St Georges Av RM17 12 B4
St Giles Cl RM16 9 F3
St James Av East
  SS17 18 D3
St James Av West
  SS17 18 D3
St Johns Mws SS17 19 E3
St Johns Rd RM16 13 G4
St Johns Way SS17 19 E3
St Leonards Cl RM17 11 G6
St Margarets Av SS17 18 B6
St Marys Cl RM17 12 C5
St Marys Rd RM16 13 G3
St Michaels Cl RM15 4 E3
St Michaels Rd RM16 13 G4
St Patricks Pl RM16 13 G3
St Pauls Cl RM15 4 E2
St Pauls Pl RM15 4 E2
St Peters Rd RM16 13 G3
St Teresa Walk RM16 13 F3
St Thomas's Pl RM17 3 E2
Saints Walk RM16 13 G3
Saladin Dr RM19 5 B6
Salisbury Av SS17 18 B5
Salisbury Rd RM17 3 E2
Salix Rd RM17 12 C6
Samphire Cl RM17 12 D6
San Juan Dr RM20 11 E4
San Luis Dr RM20 11 E4
San Marcos Dr RM20 11 E4
Sanctuary Gdns SS17 18 D4
Sandhurst Rd RM18 15 G3
Sandringham Cl SS17 18 D3
Sandy La,
  Aveley RM15 4 B2
Sandy La,
  Chadwell St Mary
  RM16 13 G6
Sandy La,
  West Thurrock RM20 10 D5
Santiago Way RM20 11 E5
Sawstone Ct*,
  Linnet Way RM19 5 D7
School La RM16 9 F4
Schoolfield Rd RM20 16 D1
Scilla Ct RM17 12 C6
Scott Rd RM16 13 F4
Scratton Rd SS17 18 B5
Seaborough Rd
  RM16 13 G3
Seabrooke Rise RM17 3 C3
Seally Rd RM17 3 B2
Second Av,
  Grays RM20 10 C5
Second Av,
  Stanford-le-Hope
  SS17 18 C3
Sedge Ct RM17 12 C6
Selwyn Rd RM18 15 E3
Semper Rd RM16 13 G2
Semples SS17 19 E4
Severn RM18 17 C3
Severn RM15 4 E1

Sewell Cl RM20 10 D5
Sexton Rd RM18 15 E2
Seymour Rd RM18 14 D2
Shakespeare Av
  RM18 15 G2
Shannon Way RM15 4 D2
Shaw Cres RM18 15 G2
Sheldon Cl SS17 19 G2
Shelley Pl RM18 15 G1
Sherfield Rd RM17 3 C3
Sheringham Cl SS17 18 D3
Sherwood RM16 11 F1
Ship La RM15,19 4 F4
Shorewell Ct*,
  Oakhill Rd RM19 5 D7
Siddons Cl SS17 17 B2
Silverdale SS17 18 B3
Silverdale East SS17 18 C2
Silverlocke Rd RM17 12 B6
Silvertown Av SS17 18 C4
Silverwood Cl RM16 7 H6
Simmons Pl RM18 11 H1
Sleepers Farm Rd
  RM16 13 G2
Solway RM18 17 C3
Somerset Rd SS17 17 B2
Sorrel Ct RM17 12 C6
South Hill SS17 20 C6
South Hill Cres SS17 20 C6
South Par RM15 6 D4
South Rd SS17 6 D3
South Vw RM16 9 F3
Southend Rd,
  Grays RM17 12 B3
Southend Rd,
  Stanford-le-Hope
  SS17 18 B5
Southey Walk RM18 15 G2
Southgate Rd RM19 5 E6
Southview Rd RM18 15 F2
Southview Rd RM20 10 D5
Southwell Rd RM20 10 D5
Speedwell Ct RM17 12 D6
Spencer Walk RM18 15 F2
Spindles RM18 15 F2
Springfield Rd RM16 12 C1
Springhouse La SS17 19 E5
Springhouse Rd SS17 18 D2
Squirrels Chase RM16 13 E2
Stafford Cl,
  Grays RM16 10 D3
Stafford Cl,
  Stanford-le-Hope
  SS17 17 B2
Stanford Gdns RM15 4 F3
Stanford Hall SS17 19 E3
Stanford Rd,
  Grays RM17 12 C2
Stanford Rd,
  Stanford-le-Hope
  SS17 18 A6
Stanford-Le-Hope By-Pass
  SS17 18 A5
Stanley Rd,
  Grays RM17 3 C2
Stanley Rd,
  Upminster RM14 20 B2
Station App RM17 3 B3
Station Rd,
  Gravesend DA11 14 A4
Station Rd,
  Tilbury RM18 17 A6
Stenning Av RM18 17 B4
Stephens Cres SS17 20 C5
Stephenson Av RM18 15 F2
Stifford Clays Rd
  RM16 8 A6
Stifford Hill RM16 7 E6
Stifford Rd RM15 6 A6
Stone Ness Rd RM20 16 E1
Stonehouse La RM20 10 A4
Stonehouse Rd RM19 5 F7
Storas Ct*,
  Linnet Way RM19 5 D7
Stour Rd RM16 13 E4
Stratford Gdns SS17 18 C4
Strathmore RM18 17 C3
Struan Av SS17 18 D1
Stuart Rd RM17 3 C1
Sullivan Rd RM18 15 F1
Sundew Ct RM17 12 C6

Swale Cl RM15 4 E2
Swallow Cl RM16 10 D4
Swiftsure Rd RM16 10 D3
Swinburne Gdns
  RM18 15 G2
Sycamore Cl RM18 15 G2
Sycamore Way RM15 7 E2
Sydney Rd RM18 15 E3
Sylvan Cl RM16 11 F3
Syringa Ct RM17 12 C6

Taits SS17 19 E4
Tallis Cl SS17 18 B3
Talus RM19 5 F6
Tamar Dr RM15 4 E2
Tamarisk Rd RM15 6 D1
Tank Hill Rd RM19 5 B6
Tank La RM16 5 B6
Tasker Rd RM16 13 G3
Tasman Cl SS17 19 E2
Templer Av RM16 13 E3
Tennants Row RM18 14 D3
Tennyson Av RM17 12 A3
Tennyson Walk RM18 15 G2
Teviot RM15 4 E2
Thackeray Av RM18 15 G1
Thames Cl SS17 19 E3
Thames Cres SS17 19 G1
Thames Dr RM16 13 F5
Thames Gateway
  RM19 4 A3
Thames Haven Rd
  SS17 19 F3
Thames Ind Pk
  RM18 17 B5
Thames Rd RM17 3 C4
Thames Vw RM16 13 F5
Thamley RM19 5 C6
The Acres SS17 18 D4
The Avenue SS17 19 H1
The Beeches RM18 15 G2
The Chase RM20 11 E6
The Circle RM18 15 F2
The Close RM16 12 A1
The Creek DA11 14 A6
The Drewe RM17 3 B3
The Firs RM16 8 B6
The Geerings SS17 18 D1
The Glade Bsns Centre
  RM20 10 B5
The Glen SS17 18 D4
The Green,
  Grays RM16 9 F3
The Green,
  South Ockendon RM157 E1
The Green,
  Stanford-le-Hope
  SS17 18 B5
The Griffins RM16 12 A2
The Grove SS17 18 B6
The Haven RM16 13 E4
The Hawthorns SS17 19 H2
The Hollies SS17 18 B5
The Limes RM19 5 B6
The Mall RM17 3 C2
The Manorway SS17 18 B4
The Mews RM17 12 B4
The Mount SS17 19 E4
The Paddocks RM16 9 F3
The Parade RM15 4 E4
The Pines RM16 12 A1
The Precinct SS17 18 B5
The Quadrant RM19 5 E6
The Retreat RM19 3 D3
The Rookery RM20 10 C6
The Rowans RM15 4 E3
The Shore DA11 14 B6
The Sorrells SS17 18 D4
The Spinney RM16 9 F3
The Square SS17 20 C5
The Sycamores RM15 4 E3
The Tyrells SS17 19 E3
The Willows RM17 12 C5
Theobalds Av RM17 3 F1
Third Av, Grays RM20 10 B6
Third Av,
  Stanford-le-Hope
  SS17 18 C2
Thomas Bata Av
  RM18 14 D3
Thorley Rd RM16 11 H1

Thors Oak SS17 18 C4
Thurloe Walk RM17 11 H3
Thurrock Bsns Centre
  RM20 10 B6
Thurrock Commercial
  Centre RM19 4 A4
Thurrock Enterprise Pk
  RM17 3 A2
Thurrock Parkway
  RM18 14 C1
Timber Ct RM17 3 B4
Titan Way RM17 3 B1
Toft Av RM17 12 C3
Tomkins Cl SS17 18 B4
Toplands Av RM15 4 D3
Toronto Rd RM18 15 E3
Torridge RM18 17 C3
Towers Rd RM17 3 F1
Trent RM18 17 D4
Tripat Cl SS17 19 H1
Triumph Cl RM16 11 E4
Tudor Av SS17 18 D2
Tunnel Cotts RM20 10 C6
Tunnel Ind Est
  RM20 10 A4
Turners Row RM17 3 F2
Turnpike La RM18 13 H4
Turold Rd SS17 18 D2
Turp Av RM16 12 B2
Tweed RM18 17 D3
Tyne RM18 17 D3
Tyne Gdns RM15 4 E2
Tyrrells Hall Cl RM17 12 C5
Tyssen Pl RM15 6 D1

Upton Cl SS17 18 C4
Usk Rd RM15 4 E1

Valmar Av SS17 18 A6
Verbena Cl RM15 6 D5
Vexil Cl RM19 5 F6
Vicarage Sq RM17 3 B3
Victoria Av RM16 12 B1
Victoria Cl RM16 12 B1
Victoria Rd,
  Horndon on the Hill
  SS17 20 B5
Victoria Rd,
  Stanford-le-Hope
  SS17 18 B5
Victoria Rd,
  Upminster RM14 20 B3
Victory Cl RM16 11 E4
Victory Rd RM20 11 E4
Vigerons Way RM16 13 G4
Vincent Av SS17 20 C5
Vincent Cl SS17 19 F3
Viola Cl RM15 6 D2

Waldon RM18 17 C3
Walkers Sq SS17 18 C5
Wallace Rd RM17 11 H3
Wallis Pk DA11 14 A6
Walpole Ct RM17 12 B4
Walsham Enterprise Pk
  RM17 3 F2
Waltons Hall Rd SS17 17 B1
Warburtons SS17 19 E4
Ward Av RM17 12 A3
Warren Cl SS17 18 C6
Warren Heights RM16 11 F3
Warren La RM16 11 E4
Warren Ter RM16 11 F2
Warwick Pl DA11 14 A6
Water La RM19 5 C6
Waterglade Ind Pk
  RM20 10 B5
Waterson Rd RM16 13 G4
Watson Cl RM20 16 D3
Watts Cres RM19 5 E6
Waverley Gdns RM16 11 H1
Wayfaring Grn RM17 3 A1
Waymans RM15 4 E1
Webster Rd SS17 18 D5
Weelkes Cl SS17 18 B3
Well La RM16 7 G6
Welland RM18 17 D3
Welling Rd RM16 9 H5
Wellington Ct RM16 12 A1
Wellington Rd RM18 15 F3
Wennington Rd RM13 4 A2

Wentworth Pl RM16 12 B2
West Rd RM15 6 C1
West St,
  Gravesend DA12 15 F6
West St, Grays RM17 3 B3
West Thurrock Relief Rd
  RM20 10 A6
West Thurrock Way
  RM20 10 B4
Westland Vw RM16 7 H6
Weston Av RM20 10 A6
Weydale SS17 19 F1
Wharf Cl SS17 18 B6
Wharf Rd,
  Grays RM17 3 A3
Wharf Rd,
  Stanford-le-Hope
  SS17 18 B5
Wharf Rd South RM17 3 A3
Wheatley Rd SS17 19 F1
Wheelers La SS17 19 H1
Whitebeam Dr RM15 7 E2
Whitehall La SS17 3 F2
Whitehall Rd RM17 12 B4
Whitfields SS17 18 D4
Whitmore Av RM16 8 A6
Whitwell Ct SS17 18 B6
Whybrews SS17 19 E4
Wickham Rd RM16 13 G2
Wilde Cl RM18 15 G3
William St RM17 3 E3
Williamsons Way
  SS17 19 E1
Willow Hill SS17 18 D1
Wills Hill SS17 18 C4
Wilsman Rd RM15 7 E1
Wilson Cl SS17 18 B6
Windsor Av,
  Grays RM16 12 A1
Windsor Av,
  Stanford-le-Hope
  SS17 19 E1
Wingfield RM17 11 G4
Wingrove Dr RM19 5 C7
Wokingdon Rd RM16 13 G3
Wood Av RM19 5 D6
Wood St RM17 3 F3
Woodbrooke Way
  SS17 19 F1
Woodcutters Av
  RM16 12 A2
Woodlands Cl RM16 12 D2
Woodmanhurst Rd
  RM20 12 C3
Woodview RM16,17 12 C3
Woodward Heights
  RM17 12 A4
Woolf Walk RM18 15 G3
Woolifers Av SS17 19 F2
Worcester Cl SS17 18 B6
Wordsworth Cl RM18 15 G3
Worthing Cl RM17 11 F6
Wouldham Rd RM17 11 F6
Wren Walk RM18 15 F1
Wroxall Ct*,
  Linnet Way RM19 5 D7

York Av SS17 19 E1
York Rd SS17 20 B5